DELAWARE WATER GAP

NATIONAL RECREATION AREA

MICHAEL P. GADOMSKI

SCHIFFER PUBLISHING

4880 Lower Valley Road · Atglen, PA 19310

Other Schiffer Books by the Author:
The Poconos: Pennsylvania's Mountain Treasure, ISBN 978-0-7643-4924-9
Scenes from the Country Fair, ISBN 978-0-7643-5480-9
Reserves of Strength: Pennsylvania's Natural Landscape, ISBN 978-0-7643-4422-0
Pittsburgh: A Renaissance City, ISBN 978-0-7643-4923-2
Pennsylvania: A Portrait of the Keystone State, ISBN 978-0-7643-5107-5
Philadelphia: Portrait of a City, ISBN 978-0-7643-5108-2
Pittsburgh: A Keepsake, ISBN 978-0-7643-5758-9
Philadelphia: A Keepsake, ISBN 978-0-7643-5757-2

Other Schiffer Books on Related Subjects:
Delaware River Reflections, Daniel Will, ISBN 978-0-7643-5229-4

Copyright © 2019 by Michael P. Gadomski

Library of Congress Control Number: 2018958777

Designed by Jack Chappell
Cover design by Molly Shields

Type set in Avance/Geometr415/Geometr706/Cambria

ISBN: 978-0-7643-5753-4
Printed in China

Published by Schiffer Publishing, Ltd.
4880 Lower Valley Road
Atglen, PA 19310
Phone: (610) 593-1777; Fax: (610) 593-2002
E-mail: Info@schifferbooks.com
Web: www.schifferbooks.com

For our complete selection of fine books on this and related subjects, please visit our website at www.schifferbooks.com. You may also write for a free catalog.

Schiffer Publishing's titles are available at special discounts for bulk purchases for sales promotions or premiums. Special editions, including personalized covers, corporate imprints, and excerpts, can be created in large quantities for special needs. For more information, contact the publisher.

We are always looking for people to write books on new and related subjects. If you have an idea for a book, please contact us at proposals@schifferbooks.com.

DEDICATION

This book is dedicated to all the men and women of the National Park Service who tirelessly protect, preserve, maintain, and interpret "America's Best Idea" for all of us now, for future generations, and for all the world's visitors to our shores.

FOREWORD

The Delaware Water Gap National Recreation Area is a gem among the Pocono Mountains in northeastern Pennsylvania and northwestern New Jersey, with nearly 70,000 acres preserved forever for local residents and visitors to enjoy the great outdoors. There are so many things to do, such as hiking, fishing, hunting, birding, swimming, boating, canoeing, kayaking, picnicking, river camping, and exploring geology. It also offers scenic vistas, waterfalls, wildlife, wild plants, historic buildings, environmental education, Native American history, panoramic views, a leisurely drive through a natural setting, and more.

Formed over fifty years ago, the Delaware Water Gap National Recreation Area helps ensure that there will always be a natural place for all of us to enjoy. Much of the landscape is similar to what Native Americans experienced with their fervent reverence for the land and the natural world. The park connects people with our proud heritage and the natural world we all share. There is a misconception that a national recreation area is somehow less of a "park" than a national park, but this is not the case. A designated national recreation area affords the same protections and regulations as a national park but also allows some consumptive uses, such as hunting. The Delaware Water Gap National Recreation Area is only one of the over four hundred of America's favorite places that the National Park Service preserves. The Delaware Water Gap National Recreation Area provides the opportunity for visitors to be inspired.

As an avid fly angler, I've fished the Delaware River and its many tributaries in the park. The Delaware River is a fishing destination for visitors from near and far. It provides a great setting with its many fishing opportunities, magnificent scenery, and serenity. There are many waters within the park where a person can enjoy peace and solitude with nature and not see another person all day. Spending a day fishing in the park gives one an opportunity to experience the treasures that abound in this vast natural area. To quote Henry David Thoreau, "Many men go fishing all their lives not knowing it is not fish they are after."

I've visited many areas in my quest for trout fishing throughout the local area and faraway places. I've often thought that pictures cannot do full justice to the glory of nature, but Mike has managed to capture the magnificence of the park in vivid and spectacular splendor. His pictures are the next best thing to being there.

The photography in this book celebrates the wondrous scenery and treasures of the Delaware Water Gap National Recreation Area. It re-creates places and moods on film and gives us the opportunity to stop and enjoy the majesty of one of America's great places. Some pictures are of familiar places, capturing the iconic features of the Delaware Water Gap with unique perspectives. Other pictures are of less popular areas, places where very few people have visited. Some pictures reveal the subtle beauty of common features such as wildflowers, trees, and landscapes in amazing colors, which encourages us to take a closer look at marvels we might miss while passing by. This book provides an awareness of the spiritual associations found in nature where God has shed His grace on us.

Whether we are armchair nature lovers, occasional hikers, or hardcore naturalists, this book provides the opportunity to take pause and enjoy the beauty, wonder, and inspiration interpreted in these photographs. It is a celebration of rich and diverse features and provides a greater awareness of the significance of the park. I am very fortunate to have had the privilege of working in the Delaware Water Gap Natural Recreation Area.

William L. Leonard Jr.
Retired Deputy Superintendent
Delaware Water Gap
National Recreation Area

ACKNOWLEDGMENTS

I would like to thank the staff at Delaware Water Gap National Recreation Area for the assistance, guidance, and encouragement given to me during the production of this book, especially John J. Donahue, William L. Leonard Jr., Carla Beasley, Kathleen Sandt, and Laura Bruce.

I also want to thank my wife, "Smitty," for again proofreading my somewhat dyslexic writing and for throwing those frozen pizzas in the oven at the last minute.

INTRODUCTION

The warm summer afternoon brings puffy, towering cumulus clouds billowing to tremendous heights in a deep-blue azure sky. I'm in my kayak effortlessly floating down the river as the gentle current takes me past riverbanks lined with giant sycamore and silver maple trees. The river often curves and divides around pristine natural islands. Except for a few other kayakers and a canoeist, no other signs of human activity are in sight. Great blue herons fly ahead of my approach, landing farther downriver. When my kayak reaches their new location, once again they repeat their short flight downriver. I look down into the crystal-clear water beneath me and see acres of yellowish-green eelgrass gracefully swaying and dancing in the current like the grass on a Polynesian hula dancer's skirt. Everything around me is still and peaceful. Suddenly, a loud, piercing shrill breaks the silence. I look up to see a majestic bald eagle flying directly over me, heading upriver.

I'll admit it; I'm a pretty darn lucky guy! Not lucky in the sense of finding or winning lots of money, since I never play the lottery and have actually never been inside a casino. Every year when I get the Publishers Clearing House Sweepstakes promotion in the mail it goes right in the trash, unopened. I always buckle my car's seat belt, try never to speed, never text and drive, and never ever drink and drive, always avoiding chancing my luck.

But I'm lucky in other ways. I can jump in my car and within forty minutes be in one of the most unique and diverse units of the National Park Service. It's a place where I can observe and photograph lizards and a species of cactus similar to those found in the Southwest, giant old-growth conifers (a few as old as the nation itself), glacially carved lakes, waterfalls galore (including the largest in two states), and historic sites that could fill several volumes of literature, many predating the French and Indian War. I can then get in my kayak and float down thirty-seven miles on one of the very few remaining undammed, free-flowing rivers in the eastern United States and glide right to a geological feature that was once touted as one of the scenic wonders of the world.

I share my good fortune with over thirty million other people who live within a two-hour drive of this priceless and vital natural gem, the Delaware Water Gap National Recreation Area. In a rare combination of three National Park Service units, encompassed within the recreation area are the Middle Delaware Scenic and Recreational River and nearly twenty-six miles of the world-renowned Appalachian National Scenic Trail.

I started visiting and taking photographs here in 1965, around the time Congress designated the land for the proposed (and now deauthorized) Tocks Island Reservoir. Most of the land was still privately owned at that point. Childs Park, which is now part of the Delaware Water Gap National Recreation Area, was then part of the Pennsylvania State Park system and known as George W. Childs State Park. I made several visits there, photographing the waterfalls, Dingmans Creek, and old-growth conifers. In those days I was mostly shooting in black and white, both 35 mm and medium format, with an occasional 35 mm color slide.

Partly frozen Fulmar Falls in Pennsylvania's former George W. Childs State Park, circa 1970.

A few years later, I began working for April Photo Center in Mount Pocono as a resort photographer. April Photo Center was the largest of the Pocono Mountain photography businesses that served the then-massive post– World War II resort industry in the Poconos. I was one of the six to eight April Photo Center photographers who would go out to the contracted resorts and photograph the guests during their stay and then provide them with professionally made prints as keepsakes of their vacation.

One of the resorts that I was assigned to was Honeymoon Haven in Dingmans Ferry, which years later became the Pocono Environmental Education Center in the national recreation area. While at Honeymoon Haven I would photograph the newlyweds as they enjoyed their honeymoon: sitting with their new friends in the dining room, bowling, swimming at the pool, delighting in a quiet, romantic moment on the grounds, dancing in the nightclub, or voluntarily being under the spell of the entertainment hypnotist who would visit weekly. Honeymoon Haven became my favorite resort, not only for its casual and laid-back atmosphere, but also because of the very friendly and welcoming staff, many of whom were local longtime residents of the area.

One of my favorite activities to photograph while at the resort was the weekly trip (during the snow-free months) to George W. Childs State Park. "Smoky," Honeymoon Haven's social director, would load up the resort's rickety old 1950s-era school bus with a dozen or so honeymoon couples, and off we would fly across the then-seldom-used dirt backroads, over hills and around curves. Smoky would sometimes "put the pedal to the medal," making the trip a thrill ride in itself, with the riders screaming or laughing hysterically nearly the entire way to the park.

The first stop at the park, after some of the riders' urgent use of the primitive outhouse restroom facilities, possibly due in part to the bus ride, was Factory Falls. One by one, each couple stood on the large, flat rock at the base of the falls, and I would photograph each couple in a variety of poses: embracing facing the camera, looking in each other's eyes, kissing, the groom holding the bride in his arms, the bride holding the groom in her arms, and whatever else spontaneously happened. From there, the couples wandered the trails on their own, enjoying the other two waterfalls and the magnificent hemlock and white pine forest. The bus ride back to the resort was a little more relaxed and reserved, as everyone seemed rather tired, yet inspired, from their afternoon in the wild.

A few years later, I was hired by the Pennsylvania Bureau of State Parks as a park naturalist at Promised Land State Park, located about sixteen miles east of George W. Childs State Park. At that time George W. Childs State Park was administered by Promised Land State Park, and on a few occasions I led guided nature walks through "Childs Park," as we called it. Occasionally during these walks we would run into Ollie Ryder, park foreman, and I would try to persuade him to share with the group some of his extensive knowledge and experiences of Childs Park. Unfortunately, Ollie, being more of the quiet and shy type, could never be persuaded.

After George W. Childs State Park was transferred to the National Park Service in 1983 and renamed George W. Childs Recreation Site, I continued visiting and photographing this spectacular natural area. By this time much of the Delaware Water Gap National Recreation Area had been firmly established, and along with the waterfalls at Childs, I had Raymondskill Falls, Dingmans and Silverthread Falls, Hackers Falls, and Buttermilk Falls to add to my increasing collection of waterfall photographs.

One spring day, I was privileged to photograph a prescribed burn in the Freeman Tract of the park. The purpose of the intentionally ignited fire was severalfold—to clear a seventy-acre former agriculture field of nonnative invasive plants, maintain the scenic or historical landscape, remove accumulated flammable vegetative material to prevent larger wildfires, and promote the growth of native grassland plants. Many other areas had also been planned to be burned that spring. However, the weather conditions and advancing spring season gave a window for only this particular burn to occur that year. Everything had to be just right.

Around noon, crews not only from the National Park Service but also from several other departments began to stage in one of the parking areas. While waiting for everyone to arrive, I had a chance to chat awhile and catch up on old times with my longtime friend, Shawn Turner, forest fire specialist supervisor with the Pennsylvania Bureau of Forestry. Shawn and others from the Bureau of Forestry were there to assist with the burn.

When everyone had arrived, the twenty or so highly trained fire professionals assembled in a semicircle. The burn boss addressed the group, going over every detail imaginable to aid them in their coming task. The current weather conditions from several different nearby coordinates were obtained and read to the group. The terrain they would be entering was described in detail, and the present species, communication procedures, smoke management, control of sightseers, objectives of the particular burn, and of course all safety rules and procedures were covered again. I could not think of one detail that wasn't covered.

The group then broke up into two separate preassigned crews: the firing crew, which would be igniting the fire, and the holding crew, which would be containing the fire within the prescribed boundary. Again, both crews were reminded of their specific tasks, and all safety procedures were reviewed, as were the resource management objectives.

When everyone was ready and suited up with safety gear and clothing, all members individually took their specific equipment and in single file advanced through the perimeter of the burn site to their assigned duty locations. While waiting for the burn to start, a few members of the crew took one last walk through sections of the field, looking for any new hazards or wildlife. A wood turtle was found and moved to a safe area out of the burn site near the river.

The burn boss, along with a couple of his assistants, again assessed the location, current weather, and wind conditions. When everything seemed just right, the burn boss carefully and precisely dripped a few drops of flaming fuel from his driptorch on the dry vegetation. A small patch of vegetation ignited. The burn boss carefully studied its behavior and slow advance. When he was satisfied everything was working as planned, he made a few other drops from his driptorch along the perimeter of the overgrown field. My training in wildfires when I worked for the Pennsylvania Bureau of State Parks was very limited, since I was mostly a first responder and more involved with traffic control and public safety, so I thought it was rather odd that the fire was started on the leeward, or downwind, side of the field. However, it soon became very evident to me that this was to clear out all burnable material before the main fire began. Slowly, a low column of fire crept upwind across the field, clearing a firebreak, or control line, several yards deep. Other small fires were started on the edges of the field to create other control lines. When it seemed to be going exactly as planned, and more than adequate firebreaks had been established on three sides of the field, the windward side was ignited. Aided by the gentle wind, this fire advanced quickly into the field.

One member of the holding crew who knew I was inexperienced in prescribed burns said to me, "Watch this, it will rear up and then go right down." And he was right! The fire became more intense, and soon a tornado-like whirlwind of flame shot up about twenty-five feet in the middle of the field. For a few moments it looked like everything was out of control, and then suddenly, quicker than it began, the fire subsided to only a few small, smoldering pockets. As these pockets were burning out, the holding crew circled the outer perimeter of the fire, checking for and immediately extinguishing any tiny burning pockets that may have jumped the perimeter. They call this mopping up. In a short time, what had been an overgrown, seventy-acre weedy field full of invasive nonnative plants became a blackened carpet of tiny scattered pockets of smoke, which one by one soon died out.

After the fire, I asked Michael Guarinoi, NPS engine foreman, why they call it a "prescribed burn" instead of a "controlled burn." He explained to me that they write a scientifically based prescription for the fire, taking in all factors, including possible side effects, just like a medical doctor would write a prescription for a patient. If all is right, and everything *must* be right for the burn crew, they will go ahead with the burn, with the primary intent of improving the overall health of the location. A controlled burn, on the other hand, is just containing a fire without taking in all the factors and outcomes.

The next day, I returned to the burn site. Everything was peaceful. The ground was cool and there was no sign of fire or smoke. The woody, nonnative invasive plants stood as charred sticks in a blackened landscape. The outline of the fire was precise, as though someone had drawn the perimeter by using a giant ruler or straight edge. Outside the perimeter, the neighboring vegetation was unscathed and taking on the rich, green color of spring.

Three months passed until I visited the site again. When I arrived, I was shocked to see that what just ninety days earlier had been a field looking outwardly devastated was now densely covered with native grasses and other herbaceous vegetation. The dominant plant was big bluestem, *Andropogon gerardi*, a very desirable native grass used by numerous species of birds for food and cover, as well as other types of wildlife. I tried to photograph the sea of grass, but it was well over my head. I had to return a few weeks later with a small stepladder to stand on to get even a respectable photograph across the field.

While many people now understand the importance of these prescribed burns, there are still some who question why they are done. They might see it as some form of destruction or interference and instead want to see nature "left alone." After all, most of us were brought up with Smokey Bear telling us to prevent fires. Part of the National Park Service mandate is "to conserve the scenery and the natural and historic objects and the wildlife therein." Much of the "natural scenery" we see today is nowhere near what existed in pre-Columbian times. Nonnative plants and animals have invaded the landscape and, in many places, have forced out the native plants. When native plants are diminished, the native wildlife that depends on them also decreases. Prescribed burns are one of the most effective tools, both in costs and results, for reducing these nonnative invasive plants and in turn creating favorable habitat for native wildlife. Additionally, low-intensity prescribed burns reduce the stockpile of flammable dried vegetation and the possibility of large, out-of-control wildfires.

From a historical perspective, fire has for the most part been a naturally occurring event in many ecosystems. In addition, through well-documented evidence it is known that the original Native Americans who occupied the area used fire for thousands of years, not only to clear land for agriculture but also to provide wildlife habitat and favorable conditions for certain fruit-bearing plants to grow and prosper. This was vital for their subsistence and survival. Through these thousands of years, since the retreat of the glaciers after the last Ice Age, a fire-dependent grassland ecosystem evolved next to the woodland ecosystem. By using these prescribed burns, the National Park Service is conserving the scenery, the natural and historic objects, and the wildlife.

Although we can never have a natural landscape as it existed during pre-Columbian times, this at least gets us closer. We will never again see the huge flocks of passenger pigeons that once migrated over the river valley or rested in the forest, consuming the autumn mast crop of acorns, chestnuts, and beechnuts. The most populous bird species in North America, and maybe the world, is now gone forever due to overharvesting by market hunters and loss of habitat. Also gone forever is the heath hen that occupied the scrub oak / heath barrens on the ridges of the park. The thousands, or possibly millions, of huge Atlantic sturgeon that once spawned in the river have now faded into history. The once-abundant and important American chestnut has now been reduced to short-lived sprouts due to an introduced blight. With the extermination of large predators such as mountain lions and wolves, there is no natural population control for the white-tailed deer, making hunting necessary to prevent habitat damage through overbrowsing by the deer.

There are places I have hiked in Delaware Water Gap National Recreation Area where I feel as though I'm the first human to ever set foot in this magnificent natural area. Yet, I am not the first, nor will I be the last. Archaeologists have discovered that humans have been in the middle Delaware River valley for over twelve thousand years, just after the last glaciers left northern Pennsylvania and New Jersey. Over many centuries, peat has been accumulating in the nearby Pocono peat bogs. Pollen from the surrounding forest trees has also been accumulating and was preserved in the oxygen-poor peat. By examining this pollen through radioactive-carbon testing, scientists have determined that the area's climate changed many times after the Ice Age: from cold-moist to cold-dry to warm-moist to warm-dry, until it reached its current state, which has been somewhat stable for the past two thousand years or so, until recently. The native plants and animals living in the area changed with the climate, as did the ways of the Native Americans. At first they were mostly nomadic hunters and gatherers. Over the years they began to wander less and took advantage of the wild foods found locally, until around two thousand years ago when they began farming the fertile river valley soil on land they cleared with the aid of fires.

They called themselves the Lenape, or Lenni Lenape. Lenni means "genuine, pure, real, original" and Lenape means "Indian" or "man." The historical land area they inhabited was called "Lenapehoking" or "Land of the Lenape" and included what is now eastern Pennsylvania, all of New Jersey, northern Delaware, eastern New York, and a small section of Connecticut. Those who lived in what is now the park area spoke the Munsee dialect, and they called the Delaware River valley the Minisink. They lived in groups of around fifty to seventy-five people, although some lived in larger villages of around two hundred people. They had matrilineal clans, with the children belonging to the mother's clan and ancestry traced through the female line. The families were matrilocal, with newlywed couples residing with the bride's family, where her sisters and mother helped with tending to the growing family.

The Lenape were peaceful people, and after Henry Hudson encountered them in 1609 he wrote, "The natives are a very good people; for when they saw I would not remain, they supposed that I was afraid of their bows and taking the arrows, they broke them in pieces and threw them into the fire."

With the arrival of Europeans, the Lenape became known as the "Delaware," which is not of Native American origin, but rather the English name of the river, which was named for Thomas West, 3rd Baron De La Warr, the first governor of the Province of Virginia. Although early Swedish settlers referred to the Lenape as the "Renappi," the name "Delaware" stuck. At first, the arrival of Europeans opened up new trade for the original people, but soon conflicts broke out over land ownership. Then Old World diseases, for which the Lenape had no immunity, quickly spread through the people, devastating the population. When William Penn arrived in his American colony in 1682, the Lenape population had been reduced by disease, famine, and war to an approximate meager 10 percent of their former size. Through continuing conflicts with an increasing European population settling in Lenapehoking, the Lenape in the 1700s either voluntarily or, more commonly, were forcefully moved westward. Most Lenape today reside in Oklahoma, and a few communities also exist in Wisconsin and Ontario, Canada. Some individuals and families later returned and now live in their native ancestral land again.

There are countless small cemeteries within the Delaware Water Gap National Recreation Area, some privately owned and some on federal property. Many of the burial sites of the Native Americans will never be known. One of the oldest cemeteries of European descendant settlers is located off Old Mine Road in New Jersey and contains the grave of Mrs. Anna Symmes, who died twenty-one days after the signing of the Declaration of Independence and one year after giving birth to her second daughter. This daughter, also named Anna, later married William Henry Harrison, who years afterward became the ninth president of the United States, and Anna Symmes posthumously became the mother-in-law of a United States president. Harrison died of pneumonia just thirty-one days into his presidential term.

Many famous and notable historic figures lived and worked in what is now the Delaware Water Gap National Recreation Area, far too many to mention all of them in this book. However, one interesting person was Charles S. Peirce (1839–1914), a highly noted philosopher, physicist, and mathematician. He is credited as the father of the groundbreaking philosophy of pragmatism. His historic home, Aribe, in Milford, is now preserved and used as the office of the Delaware Water Gap National Recreation Area's Division of Research and Resource Management.

History abounds in the park, from Dutch settlers mining copper ore along the river north of the gap in 1652 to early wars such as the French and Indian War and the American Revolutionary War. The park had the Underground Railroad, river ferries, commercial logging rafts, scout camps, agriculture, the first solar-heated home in the United States, the second-largest inland resort in the mid-nineteenth century, one of the first large-scale environmental protests in modern times, famous artists, notable political figures, and even early silent-movie locations. The list continues.

During the first half of the twentieth century, the Pennsylvania side of the area was bustling with a growing resort industry, especially after World War II, while the New

Jersey side remained relatively quiet as an area of small farms with rural and somewhat remote villages. Then came mid-August 1955.

The summer of 1955 had been hot and dry. Any rain would have been welcomed. When Hurricane Connie was predicated to bring some much-needed rain, no one seemed concerned, and people rejoiced when she brought relief to the area on August 13 by dumping around seven inches of rain in the Poconos. The small creek near our home, which was usually just a trickle by August, was now so full that several of us kids were using it for whitewater tubing and having a ball. The ground had actually been so parched that the prediction of another hurricane moving into the area brought little anxiety. Hurricane Diane was supposed to be a rather meek storm in comparison to her sister Connie.

Diane entered the area in the early hours of August 18, and by the time she exited the next day on August 19 she had left up to thirteen inches of unexpected rain on the already saturated landscape, making the combination of both storms the worst flooding on record to hit the Poconos and along the Delaware River. According to government estimates, in Pennsylvania alone, 101 people lost their lives and damage was estimated at 70 million in 1955 dollars (approximately 640 million in 2017 dollars). Paradoxically, this tragic event was the genesis for the Delaware Water Gap National Recreation Area.

The story of the Tocks Island Dam project—the purchasing of land and removing the residents by the Army Corps of Engineers, the ensuing protests, and the final deauthorization of the project—is complicated and has been written about in detail in other volumes. This book is not about that story.

We all can empathize with those who lost their family homesteads, especially those who trace their ancestry in the valley back several generations. It is easily understandable that pain still lingers. At the same time, there were speculators who, at the announcement of the dam project, began purchasing parcels of land in hopes of capitalizing on and profiting from the government.

We cannot go back in time, nor does time ever stand still. Logic tells us that even if the project had never been proposed, the valley today would look nothing like it did back in 1962, when Congress authorized the Tocks Island Dam. All we have to do is to look at the massive development that has occurred to the west, just outside the park's boundary on the Pocono Plateau, and ask ourselves if this would not have happened along the river valley instead. Also, home developments had already begun on the Kittatinny Ridge next to the Appalachian Trail. The economics and methods of agriculture have changed in the past half century, and it is likely that many of the marginal farms in the valley would not have survived. Developers are known to make offers that can't be refused when big profits are in sight for them.

We can reminiscence about the past and wish things would stay the same while knowing they will and must change. On the other hand, we must preserve the relics and stories of the past so that future generations will know of their roots.

Gifford Pinchot was the first chief of the United States Forest Service and twice governor of Pennsylvania. His ancestral home in Milford, Grey Towers, is just outside the Delaware Water Gap Natural Recreation Area and is managed today as a national historic landmark by the United States Forest Service. Pinchot's vision of conservation was based on the concept of working for "the greatest good of the greatest number for the longest time."

Looking back, I can still see in my mind the farms, villages, and local businesses that existed just before the park was created. I can also remember some of the very friendly and welcoming people who lived there. But over the decades I've witnessed something else. I see a land that is once again, after several hundred years, being given back to nature. I have watched the forest grow, and I picture how in a generation or two our grandchildren and great-grandchildren will be taking their own children to a wonderful natural area. Barring any human or natural disasters, I can see them wandering in wonder through magnificent old-growth hemlock ravines and white pine forests, just like those that the Lenape knew and that astonished the early European settlers. They will be in awe seeing the numerous waterfalls that my parents had to pay an admission to see after going through the somewhat tacky souvenir shops, with their rubber tomahawks for sale that were made in some far-off Asian country. I can see future generations witnessing and learning about the people, both Native Americans and European settlers, who had lived and worked in the area. They will see a preserved and maintained land of natural diversity. Hikers, both short distance and thru-hikers, will be traversing the Appalachian Trail on the Kittatinny Ridge, wondering how many footsteps over many decades have set in the same spot as theirs. With the current positive reports about the future of shad, I see anglers witnessing spring runs that haven't been seen in over a century. As our population becomes more and more urbanized, this park, which lies so close to several major metropolitan areas, will become the vital and significant link to nature for these urbanites, so many of whom are unknowingly suffering from nature deficit disorder.

But more importantly, with our increasing population, urban sprawl, industrialization, and the dire predictions of climate change, this park will be a stronghold for many species. And it will also be a stronghold for the human population as it eases the negative effects of climate change. The investment in nature made here will be an investment in ourselves and future generations. The return on the investment made today promises to be tremendous, but only if we are committed to it. The National Park Service, although doing a tremendous job with the limited financial resources available to them, can do only so much. We must remember that this park, as well as all others, belongs to us, the people of the United States. How the park will appear in the future will depend entirely on us and our commitment to it.

I am optimistic as I see, sometime in the distant future, some people effortlessly floating down the still-pristine Delaware River in kayaks or canoes on a warm summer day, looking up at the cumulus clouds billowing above them, then having a bald eagle fly directly overhead. They'll feel the nurturing power of the earth and nature surround them. Suddenly, they'll realize that all the stress of urban life and their virtual existence in a digital world has suddenly left, and they'll individually think to themselves, "I'm a pretty darn lucky person!" Then they'll, maybe unconsciously, thank those of us in our time who made this precious moment possible for them, as we have thanked all those before us who have made this precious park a reality for us.

The rockslide on the flank of Mount Minsi is known as a talus slope. As the ledge above freezes and thaws, chunks of rocks break off, creating the talus. Viewed from a distance, the rocks appear small, yet some are the size of large boulders.

Viewed from downriver near the community of Slateford, Pennsylvania, the classic water gap comes into view. This ridge, which the Lenape referred to as "Endless Mountain," runs 237 miles from southern Pennsylvania to Kingston, New York. In New York it is called "Shawangunk Ridge"; in New Jersey, "Kittatinny"; and in Pennsylvania, "Blue Mountain."

Hikers who climb to the 1,527-foot-high summit of Mount Tammany are rewarded with a magnificent panoramic view of the Delaware Water Gap and Mount Minsi.

The rock ledges on Mount Tammany began forming five hundred million years ago, when quartz pebbles were deposited in a shallow sea and began to harden into solid rock. Over time the rock was pushed upward. As the water gap formed, these rock strata became exposed to become a monocline.

One of the most iconic views of the Delaware Water Gap is from the shoreline at Kittatinny Point Visitor Center. The 1,527-foot-high Mt. Tammany in New Jersey is on the left, and 1,463-foot-high Mt. Minsi in Pennsylvania is on the right.

A rocky shore borders the Delaware River near the former village of Pahaquarra, New Jersey. Pahaquarra is said to be a derivation of the Native American word "Phaqualong," which means "the place between mountains beside the water."

It is possible that a few of the older trees growing between the Old Mine Road and the Delaware River witnessed Civil War soldiers returning home to their farms in the river valley at the conclusion of the war.

17

Pristine forty-four-acre Sunfish Pond on the Kittatinny Ridge is the southernmost glacial tarn along the Appalachian Trail. A mid-1960s proposal to turn the lake into a pump storage facility to generate electricity was met with much opposition, including from US Supreme Court Justice William O. Douglas and the Lenni Lenape League.

Ornithologist Brian Hardiman tallies the species and number of birds of prey during the autumn hawk migration along Kittatinny Mountain at Raccoon Ridge. This provides valuable scientific data. An owl decoy is mounted on a post to attract a close flyby of the hawks. Owls and hawks are natural enemies.

Occasional grassy balds exist on the Kittatinny Ridge. These provide a unique habitat and breaks in the otherwise continuous forest. Ornithologists have noted a small number of snow buntings, an arctic bird, wintering on the balds. Other bird species use these as resting places while following the ridge during migration.

The Cooper's hawk, *Accipiter cooperii*, is a medium-sized hawk native to the North American continent. Typical prey species include songbirds and small game birds. Recently, it has become common around backyard bird feeders. It is a regular autumn migrant along the Kittatinny Ridge and nests in the park's forests.

One of the more popular day hikes is the Dunfield Creek Trail in New Jersey. Beginning at the base of Mt. Tammany, the trail follows the very scenic Dunfield Creek through a mature forest of hemlocks and hardwoods, with numerous cascades. The trail ends at Sunfish Pond.

First settled by American Revolution veteran Jacobus Van Gorden, the farm property went through several owners and changes. The last owner was Russell Eshback, who built the large barn for his modern dairy operation. Eshback also served in the Pennsylvania House of Representatives from 1958 to 1970.

The Cold Spring Farm springhouse just off River Road in Pennsylvania was built in the late nineteenth century. A stream of constantly cold water runs through the structure, which provided refrigeration for food before rural electrification in the 1930s. It is listed on the National Register of Historic Places.

A kayaker glides past the downstream end of Tocks Island. In 1962, Congress proposed that a dam be built at this site to create a forty-mile-long lake for flood control and hydroelectricity. After decades of local and national opposition, the **project was finally officially** deauthorized in 2002.

Islands play a vital role in the ecology of rivers and in our environment. In addition to being used as resting, feeding, and nesting areas for wildlife, they slow the river's current, trapping sediment and easing the effects of downstream flooding.

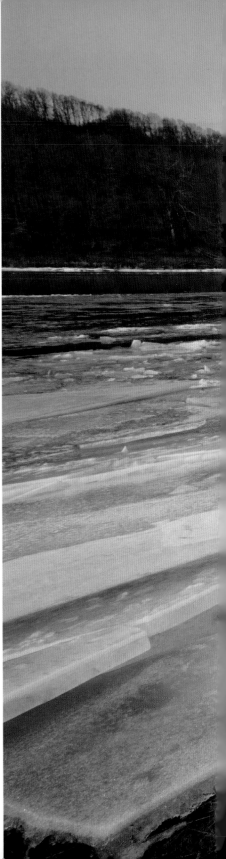

For over two decades, several hundred participants have taken part in the annual Delaware River Sojourn. Some may paddle for only one day, while others take the whole trip, lasting several days. The kayakers and canoeists experience the incredible natural resource of the Delaware River up close on a personal level.

Winter ice flows scouring the land create a unique environment along the river and the islands that ecologists refer to as the "riverside ice scour community." Here, sand and gravel bars form, which are used by shorebirds and provide habitat for the foot-high sand cherry.

Slabs of river ice replace summer sunbathers on Turtle Beach. River ice should never be considered safe to walk on, due to the unpredictable river currents underneath.

In late April, as the forest awaits the coming balmy May weather, shadbush trees will have already bloomed with their white delicate flowers, and the buds on a few trees will have opened, showing tiny immature leaves, but mostly the forest remains bare.

Bloodroot is a common early-spring wildflower growing in the park's rich woods. It is one of the few plants whose seeds are distributed by ants, in a process called myrmecochory. Although bloodroot has been used in folk medicine, this is rather dangerous because the plant is toxic to humans.

Spicebush, a deciduous shrub, is one of the earliest plants to bloom in the spring. It grows in the moist, rich forest understory. Early settlers used spicebush as an indicator of good agricultural land. When crushed, the leaves have a very fragrant, spicy, citrus-like aroma; hence its name.

Dryad's saddle fungus, *Polyporus squamosus*, is usually found growing on dead hardwood trees and can grow up to twenty inches across. Fungi play an important role in forest ecosystems by decomposing organic matter and recycling the nutrients. No mushroom should be considered safe to consume unless verified by an expert.

Top Left

Once part of a post–World War II vacation home development, Blue Mountain Lake in New Jersey is now a popular recreation area for fishing, hiking, and nature study.

Bottom Left

Built in the late nineteenth century, the Bevans-Hellwig Kitchen, along Old Mine Road, was attached to a large farmhouse. At the time the kitchen was built, the dandelions growing there were not considered lawn weeds, but rather a food source, and were used in salads, as cooked greens, and as a coffee substitute.

Bottom Center

When springtime water in the Delaware reaches 50°F, mature American shad, after spending six years at sea, begin their annual migration upriver to spawn. Once abundant, the population declined but now is increasing again. Some adults return to the sea after spawning, yet many die feeding the eagles and other wildlife.

Right

When the Delaware Water Gap National Recreation Area was established in 1965, Canada geese, *Branta canadensis*, were mainly a migrant and sometimes winter resident. However, with stocking by various state wildlife agencies, the subspecies of giant Canada goose is now a common year-round resident in much of the United States.

When the Delaware Water Gap National Recreation Area was established, many people thought it was only a matter of time until the bald eagle would be extinct in the Lower 48. Today, thanks to a ban on certain pesticides and to wise management, it is fairly common year-round in the park.

Opening buds in the park's spring
hardwood forest compete for color with
the autumn display.

Less than twenty-four hours after the burn, all embers are out and the ground is cool again. The field stands in stark contrast to the emerging spring vegetation. Most nonnative invasive plants have been destroyed. The ash will start releasing nutrients to the soil, and long-dormant seeds will come alive.

A burn boss carefully monitors the slow advance of a prescribed burn set in an overgrown field filled with nonnative invasive plants. The first fire is set in the downwind side of the field to burn off an area of vegetation, to act as a fire barrier.

During the prescribed burn, the holding crew contains the controlled fire within the prescribed boundaries. All personnel in a prescribed burn are highly trained professionals and carry the latest safety equipment. In addition to protecting the habitat, safety takes top priority.

Just four months after the prescribed burn, the field has been restored with native plants. Native big bluestem grass grows over eight feet high, and a stepladder was required to make this photograph. Other native plants, such as goldenrod, are also growing in the field, all providing excellent wildlife habitat.

Hidden on the Kittatinny Mountain is a small, unique glacial tarn called Dry Pond. It seems to be more boulder field than pond, since it has water only seasonally, often completely drying up in summer. This makes it an ideal vernal pond, vital as breeding areas for amphibians such as salamanders.

Hikers on the Blue Mountain Lake Trail can obtain a sweeping view from Indian Rocks of the Walpack Valley below and the Pocono Plateau in the far distance.

A relatively large and somewhat permanent beaver pond is found off Walpack Ridge Trail in New Jersey. These ponds provide valuable wildlife habitat.

Fifteen-acre Hemlock Pond near the top of Kittatinny Mountain is reached by hiking trails leading from Crater Lake and Blue Mountain Lake. Hikers often get a feeling of Canada here due to the pond's surrounding forest of eastern hemlock and the occasional red spruce, which is rare to the park.

Crustose and foliose lichens grow on a conglomerate rock on Kittatinny Mountain. These tiny plants are composed both of algae and fungi, living in a symbiotic relationship. They are intolerant of air pollution and will not grow in highly polluted areas. The rock's reddish-brown color may indicate traces of iron.

Allyson Schwab-Miller of the Walpack Historical
Society portrays a Victorian-era woman in the
Rosenkrans House during the annual "A Walpack
Christmas" event. Victorians rarely smiled for
a photograph.

Although some structures in Walpack Center date back to 1830, the village itself was established in 1850 and was more extensive than what is seen today. The Walpack Historical Society is headquartered and operates a museum next to the US Post Office in the First Rosenkrans House.

Of the more than a hundred miles of hiking trails in the park, plus twenty-six miles of Appalachian Trail, the most popular is probably the stroller- and wheelchair-accessible 0.3 miles of Dingmans Creek Trail. In addition to two waterfalls, the trail passes through a rhododendron thicket, excellent for spring warblers.

Possibly the most unique, yet the most easily accessed, waterfall in the park is eighty-foot-tall Silverthread Falls, located along Dingmans Creek Trail less than two hundred feet from the parking area. The falls is amply named, since it appears to be a narrow thread of water falling through the bedrock.

Most of the original, magnificent old-growth forests in New Jersey and the Poconos were cut prior to the Civil War. Yet, a few places in the park have forests that are nearing old growth, such as here along the Dingmans Creek Trail.

Beginning at the Pocono Environmental Education Center, Tumbling Waters Trail passes through deciduous and evergreen forests, two ponds, an old home site, and a beautiful thirty-foot waterfall before returning to the center to make a varied 2.8-mile round-trip hike.

The indoor pool at the former Honeymoon Haven resort is now the Pocono Environmental Education Center's Ecozone Exploration and Discovery Room. It serves as an indoor classroom, providing an opportunity to explore a beaver lodge, bat cave, eagle's nest, and fossil pit, and allows visitors to discover ecological and environmental concepts.

Several human-made and beaver-made ponds and wetlands are located off Big Egypt Road. These provide excellent habitat for numerous species of wildlife, including waterfowl and herons. The area has been designated an "Important Bird Area" by Audubon Pennsylvania.

Nearly extinct at the beginning of the twentieth century, the strikingly beautiful wood duck, *Aix sponsa*, is now a common migrant and summer resident on many of the small ponds and along some of the larger slow-flowing creeks in the park.

Scenic Upper Indian Ladder Falls, which some call Middle Falls, cascades approximately forty feet over three tiers on a shale ledge. It is one of two major waterfalls and several smaller falls on Hornbecks Creek. The waterfall is reached by hiking the 1.9-mile Hornbecks Creek Trail.

A half-mile hike off Pompey Ridge Road in New Jersey leads to the historic Richard Layton Farmhouse, which was built in two stages beginning in 1812. On July 23, 1979, it was officially listed on the National Register of Historic Places.

Mountain laurel, seen here at Crater Lake, is common throughout the park, generally growing in dry, open forest, and is in full bloom in June. It is Pennsylvania's State Flower. It's sometimes confused with rhododendron, which has larger leaves, blooms in July, and is found in moist, shaded forests.

Pitch pine is probably the hardiest tree in the park, often taking root in the tiny crack in the bedrock on Kittatinny Mountain. Exposed to weather extremes such as the hot summer sun, droughts, winter ice storms, and strong winds, it not only survives but prospers.

Hikers on the Kittatinny Ridge are often surprised to see the six-inch-long five-lined skink lizard, *Eumeces fasciatus*, scampering across the rock ledges. The blue-colored tail seen here indicates that this is an immature five-lined skink. Skinks may disconnect part of their tail to distract predators, later growing a new one.

Lower Lake Success, once part of the Blue Mountain Lakes Community development, a ten-thousand-acre mountaintop tract on Kittatinny Mountain, is now a beautiful wetland and home to beavers, waterfowl, and other wildlife.

Several pull-offs that were once seasonal home sites along Skyline Drive provide outstanding views across New Jersey's Kittatinny Valley. While here, you might hear the primeval, raspy call of a raven or see soaring turkey vultures using the ridge's rising air currents to lift them in their graceful flight.

The black bear, *Ursus americanus*, can be found on both sides of the park and possibly be encountered at any time. Although not aggressive, they are still wild animals and should remain wild. Attempting to feed a wild bear is not only unwise both for humans and bears but is also illegal.

By midsummer, the leaves on the spring wildflower called mayapple start to fade, while the fronds on Christmas fern remain green all year. Both species can be found in rich, moist forests throughout the park.

The unique, native eastern prickly pear cactus grows on the dry, warm, south-facing shale barrens on the Pennsylvania side of the park.

Located at Catfish Pond on the Kittatinny Ridge and just off the Appalachian Trail, the Mohican Outdoor Center serves as an oasis for long-distance Appalachian Trail hikers. Hikers can restock supplies, take a much-desired shower, and spend some time relaxing.

Operated by the Appalachian Mountain Club, in partnership with the National Park Service, the Mohican Outdoor Center occupies a former Boy Scout camp. Opened in 1993, the center offers cabins, campsites, and meal services through reservations for members and nonmembers of the AMC.

Thirty-one-acre Catfish Pond, near the summit of Kittatinny Mountain, is a rocky, pristine, natural glacial lake. In partnership with the National Park Service, it is now the home of the Appalachian Mountain Club's Mohican Outdoor Center.

Built around 1726, the historic Dutch Colonial Westbrook-Bell House along Old Mine Road is the oldest house in the park and the oldest still standing in Sussex County, New Jersey. It was used as a fortification during the "Border War" between the colonies of New York and New Jersey.

A 1.3-mile trail from Cliff Park Trailhead leads hikers to scenic Hackers Falls on Raymondskill Creek. Although relatively small, this picturesque falls is hidden in a rustic hemlock ravine forest. One writer said it resembles a giant faucet with gushing water.

Although many people consider the wild turkey to be a forest bird, during summer, hens will bring their poults to meadows to feed on insects and get vital protein. Nearly extinct by the early twentieth century, it has made a remarkable recovery due to stocking and habitat improvement.

Old fields that were former agriculture fields or pastures can be seen in many areas in the park. This is a transition environment and, if left alone, will succeed to shrubs, then forest in time. Yet, in the old-field stage it provides preferred habitat for some specialized species of wildlife.

The Virginia opossum, North America's only marsupial, is one of the most adaptable mammals found in the park and has been expanding its range northward. It is nonaggressive, eats almost anything, including up to five thousand ticks per season, and has a body temperature too low for rabies to survive.

The Isaac Van Campen Inn along Old Mine Road was built in 1742. Although it was a private home, because it was located along a road in an isolated area, under law it had to lodge and feed travelers. During the French and Indian War it provided protection from Indian attacks.

IN MEMORY OF
JOHN ROSENKRANS
JULY 6, 1724   JUNE 5, 1786
COLONEL OF THE SUSSEX COUNTY MILITIA
IN THE AMERICAN REVOLUTION
GRAVE 500 FEET TO THE EAST OF THIS SPOT
ERECTED BY
COL. JOHN ROSENKRANS CHAPTER, N. J. SOCIETY, S. A. R.
1958

A simple yet elegant native-stone monument along Old Mine Road near the Van Campen Inn, erected by the New Jersey Society Sons of the Revolution in 1958, honors Colonel John Rosenkrans, who served in the Third Battalion of the Sussex County Militia. The Rosenkranses have farmed this area since 1730.

At Van Campen Day, members of the Colonel Musketeers Senior Fife and Drum Corps march along the Old Mine Road. This is the same road used by many colonial troops during the French and Indian War, and again by the Continental army during the American Revolutionary War.

The gravesite of Mrs. Anna Symmes is located on a forested hill near the Van Campen Inn. Years after her death in 1777, she became the mother-in-law of President William Henry Harrison.

Standing at 1,492 feet on the Kittatinny Ridge, Rattlesnake Mountain is a bare, sunny, windswept peak along the Appalachian Trail. The summit offers fine views to the Pocono Plateau in Pennsylvania.

Late summer brings morning fog to the river valley and the delicate webs of funnel-web grass spiders. When the two combine, it is like fine lace over the meadows' low vegetation, only to disappear with the warming late-morning sun.

The historic Nelden-Roberts House was
built sometime between 1816 and 1836.
It is listed on the state historical register
in New Jersey and used as a museum by
the Montague Association for the Restoration
of Community History. Research has shown
that a small schoolhouse was also located
on the property.

Beautiful twenty-acre Thunder Mountain Lake on Walpack Ridge was once part of the three-hundred-acre Thunder Mountain Dude Ranch for boys eight to sixteen years of age. Now it is an important wildlife area. The buildings are used by the Peters Valley School of Craft for workshops in arts and crafts.

The spectacular Raymondskill Cliffs, also called the Milford Cliffs, Delaware Cliffs, or just "the Cliffs," run nearly 2.5 miles from Raymondskill Creek north to the borough of Milford. Rising 650 feet above the Delaware River, the upper 400 feet of the shale cliff form a near-vertical outcrop in places.

An old, weather-beaten, bonsai-like red cedar tree, *Juniperus virginiana*, at Tri-State Vista on the Raymondskill Cliffs has witnessed the many changes in the river valley, lying some 160 feet below.

At Bushkill, Pennsylvania, the south-flowing Delaware River makes a sharp turn and begins flowing northeast, only to make another sharp turn and flow in a southerly direction. This area is known as Walpack Bend.

Hiking the easy-to-moderate Cliff Trail provides breathtaking views not only of the river valley below, but also of three states. Several western silent-movie scenes were filmed on these cliffs in the early days of filmmaking.

The middle Delaware River has some of the best-preserved floodplain or northern riverine forests in the Northeast, with some individual trees reaching near old growth. The major trees are American sycamore, river birch, and silver maple, intercepted with vines such as wild grapes and poison ivy.

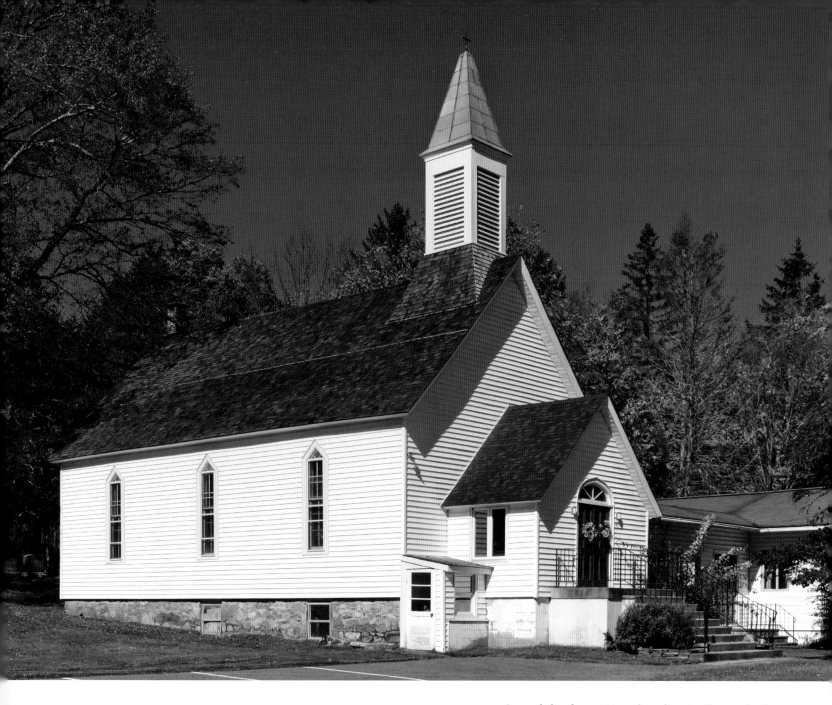

One of the few active churches in the park, the Minisink Dutch Reformed Church along River Road in Montague, New Jersey, dates its congregation back to 1737. The current church was built in 1899, with an addition built in 1959. The church and congregation are still very active today.

The shallow waters of Kittatinny Camp Lake, off Upper Ridge Road in New Jersey, make it a valuable wetland habitat for aquatic birds such as waterfowl and herons, while the surrounding shrub and woodlands provide habitat for many upland bird species.

Noted artist Marie Zimmermann (1879–1972) designed her Dutch Colonial Revival summer home south of Milford in 1910. In 1944, she closed her National Arts Club Studio in New York City to alternate her residences between Florida and Pennsylvania. This beautiful restored home is listed on the National Register of Historic Places.

Young sycamore trees reflect in the Delaware River on the upstream side of Namanock Island. This dramatic and changing environment is always in early succession. During periods of heavy flooding or powerful winter ice flows, these young trees may be uprooted and killed, only to grow back again in a few years.

Pow Wow Hill in Pennsylvania eventually rises over six hundred feet in a series of steep ledges above the Delaware River.

In addition to the stream's excellent wild-trout waters, the 0.8-mile, relatively flat, easy trail that parallels Toms Creek is a favorite for strolls and introducing children to nature. It passes through a hemlock ravine forest with scattered hardwood that adds interest and diversity.

The Pennsylvania Fish and Boat Commission has given Toms Creek its highest rating as a "Class A Wild Trout Waters," which is defined as "streams that support a population of wild (natural reproduction) trout of sufficient size and abundance to support a long-term and rewarding sport fishery."

The hemlock ravine forest is one of the most endangered ecosystems in eastern North America, mainly due to the nonnative insect called the hemlock woolly adelgid. Eastern hemlock, a foundation species, creates a forest ecosystem of dense shade with clean, cold water, vital for wildlife and downriver drinking-water supplies.

Dingmans Creek flows through a narrow chute of shale, falling approximately thirty feet into a large plunge pool to form Deer Leap Falls in George W. Childs Park. A trail above the creek allows visitors to look almost directly down the waterfall.

It is possible that more selfies have been taken in front of Factory Falls at George W. Childs Park than any other waterfalls in the East, outside of Niagara. The falls is named for the Brooks family woolen mill originally built next to the waterfalls, which operated from 1823 to 1832.

Connecting Route 560 in New Jersey and Route 739 in Pennsylvania, the circa 1889 Dingmans Ferry Bridge is the last privately owned toll bridge on the Delaware River, and one of the last left in the United States. The original bridge was built in 1837 but was destroyed in a flood.

Once a dairy farm, and then a summer residence, Loch Lomond Picnic Area contains a small lake with a pier accessible to the mobility impaired. The surrounding former agriculture fields are managed with prescribed burns to restore and maintain the historical landscape and improve habitat for native plants and wildlife.

Originating high on the Pocono Plateau at Peck's Pond in Pike County, Pennsylvania, the Bush Kill, also called Big Bushkill Creek, flows 30.1 miles before joining the Delaware River. Throughout much of its course it is noted for its fine trout fishing.

Table Rock, located just off the Appalachian Trail on the flank of Mt. Minsi, is a large, unique flat rock. Up until the early 1970s, this was reachable by automobile and was a famous tourist spot and vista. It contained parking and picnic areas, and a refreshment and souvenir pavilion.

Of the nearly two hundred lakes and ponds within the park, forty-acre Hidden Lake, near the park headquarters, may be the most popular, not only for fishing but also for picnicking, easy hiking, nature study, and nature photography, due to the scenic beauty found along its 1.9-mile loop trail.

The thirty-two-mile Pennsylvania McDade Recreational Trail is open for hiking its entire length, and for mountain and hybrid bikes most of its length. At the park headquarters the trail passes a cattail marsh that is excellent for wildlife viewing. Bobcats, black bear, and numerous bird species have been sighted here.

The Millbrook Village Methodist Episcopal Church was built in 1973 on the basis of plans of the original 1860 church. Some of the buildings in Millbrook Village are original, while others were either moved here or constructed on-site to re-create an eighteenth-century rural hamlet and demonstrate the folkways of the time.

Autumn is a wonderful time to drive some of the park's lesser-used roads, not only to enjoy the brilliant autumn foliage; those who are observant and drive at a reasonable speed might also spot some of the park's wildlife.

Van Campens Glen passes through a pristine hemlock ravine with a few small, scattered cascades. It is an excellent birding area, with several species of warblers being recorded as breeding in the glen. The glen can be slippery in places, so visitors are reminded to stay on designated trails.

Interpretive Ranger Quinn Gilly performs and demonstrates his rare, authentic Civil War–era five-string fretless banjo at the annual Millbrook Days.

The traditional technique of candle dipping is demonstrated at Millbrook Days. Once a year, neighboring housewives would get together to produce a year's supply of candles, often the only interior light source for eighteenth- and nineteenth-century rural homes.

Abram Garis built a gristmill along Van Campen Brook in 1832. Soon afterward, the village of Millbrook evolved, peaking in the 1870s. Afterward, the village declined, and the mill burned in 1922. The 1948 mill seen today was moved to its current site in the 1990s, near the original Garis Mill.

The current blacksmith shop in Millbrook Village was moved to this location in the 1970s to depict the original blacksmith shop that operated in the village until the 1950s. On weekends and during special events, a skilled blacksmith is in the shop to demonstrate this old but enduring craft.

Park volunteer Fred Schofer portrays and explains the life and work of the fur traders and trappers of the eighteenth and early nineteenth centuries at the annual Millbrook Days folklife festival.

The Millbrook Village lantern tours have become a popular event where visitors listen to stories and learn about nineteenth-century Halloween traditions and customs.

A rather typical Victorian parlor of the nineteenth-century rural middle class is seen in the restored 1859 Elias Garis House in Millbrook Village. Although historical tax records indicate that the Garis family was not particularly affluent, archaeological excavations found that they used fine china dishes and pressed glassware.

The Millbrook Village seen today is not the exact Millbrook that flourished from 1832 to 1900. Rather, it is a partly restored and re-created village depicting the farming-based hamlets found in the area during the nineteenth century. Depue Cabin, built in 1830, was moved to Millbrook in 1980.

Sandra Smith, a volunteer in parks, warms up in front of the fireplace in the Depue Cabin while interpreting the life of nineteenth-century pioneer women at Millbrook Village during "A Victorian Christmas."

When most of the deciduous trees in the park have lost their leaves and autumn is about to give up its reign to winter, river birches and silver maples along the riverbank and on islands such as Poxono still retain their brilliantly colored leaves until brought down by November gales.

Hikers on the Appalachian Trail, north of Millbrook-Blairstown Road, pass the small yet scenic Black's Pond, which often has an active beaver colony. This pond provides valuable wetland wildlife habitat near the summit of Kittatinny Mountain.

Autumn leaves and pine needles rain down into Raymondskill Creek. These leaves will be used as food by aquatic insects, which in turn will feed the fish and other animals in the stream. Nothing in nature is wasted, but all part of the food chain.

As if a preview of coming attractions, visitors driving to the Dingmans Falls Visitor Center pass a very scenic section of Dingmans Creek, with small cascades flowing through a mature forest of hemlocks and deciduous trees.

Although several hundred visitors a day may pass through the Dingmans Falls Visitor Center during the peak summer visitation period, in winter, when the road to the falls is closed, the building lies in peaceful tranquility, with the only sound being the nearby creek and the occasional black-capped chickadee calling.

Every year thousands of people visit 130-foot-high Dingmans Falls, Pennsylvania's second highest. However, few get to experience its wonder in winter. Winter conditions necessitate closure of the access road, so an approximate 1.75-mile one-way hike from Rt. 209 is required. Still, the boardwalk trail section can be icy and dangerous.

The vines of Virginia creeper, *Parthenocissus quinquefolia*, find support on the sides of an old wooden barn. It's sometimes mistaken for poison ivy, which has three leaves instead of five. Although the berries of Virginia creeper are toxic to humans, they provide an important winter food for many bird species.

Scenic sixteen-acre Crater Lake, one of the three natural glacial lakes on Kittatinny Mountain within the park, lies the farthest north. Contrary to urban legends, it was not made by a meteorite crashing to earth. Rather, it is a glacial tarn formed in a cirque excavated by a glacier.

Dropping 150 feet in three tiers, Raymondskill Falls is the highest waterfall in Pennsylvania, and only a few feet shorter than Niagara Falls. New trails and viewing platforms provide wonderful views, both from the bottom of the second tier and from above, looking down on the falls.

Tumbling approximately two hundred feet down a series of rock ledges off Kittatinny Mountain, Buttermilk Falls ranks as the highest waterfall in New Jersey. Wooden stairs and viewing platforms on the left side of the falls give hikers who make the climb unique viewpoints of the waterfall.

117

In mid-December, the first sheet of ice forms on the park's ponds. Like many other ponds, in Stuckey's Pond in Pennsylvania fish remain active under the ice, while amphibians go into hibernation in the pond's muddy bottom. Painted turtles go into a slow metabolic state and can remain active under the ice.

Around nine miles of Flat Brook flows through the Walpack Valley in the park before joining the Delaware River at River Bend near the former village of Flatbrookville. In addition to being one of New Jersey's premier trout streams, it also ranks high for bird watching.

An excellent and rewarding winter activity in the park is searching for wildlife tracks left in the snow, such as these river otter tracks found along Dingmans Creek. Much information can be learned about an animal's habits just by following their tracks.

Located in the former New Jersey village of Bevans, internationally renowned Peters Valley School of Craft, a nonprofit corporation, was founded in 1970 in partnership with the National Park Service "to promote and encourage education and excellence in craft." The Craft Store features work of three hundred artists from across the country.

Many people end their visit to the Delaware Water Gap National Recreation Area by admiring a spectacular sunset on the Delaware River.

BIBLIOGRAPHY

Abramson, Ruby, and Jean Haskell. *Encyclopedia of Appalachia*. Knoxville: University of Tennessee Press, 2006.

Allen, Peter, and Brian Cassie. *The Audubon Society Field Guide to the Mid-Atlantic States*. New York: Alfred A. Knopf, 1991.

Amos, William H. *The Life of the Pond*. New York: McGraw-Hill, 1967.

Behler, John L. *The Audubon Society Field Guide to North American Reptiles and Amphibians*. New York: Alfred A. Knopf, 1979.

Boyle, William J., Jr. *A Guide to Bird Finding in New Jersey*. New Brunswick, NJ: Rutgers University Press, 2008.

Boysen, Robert L. *Kittatinny Trails*. Mahwah, NJ: New York–New Jersey Trail Conference, 2004.

Brock, Frederic, Susan Fordyce, Dan Kunkle, and Tim Fenchel. *Eastern Pennsylvania Birding & Wildlife Guide*. Harrisburg: Pennsylvania Department of Conservation and Natural Resources, 2009.

Brooks, Maurice. *The Life of the Mountains*. New York: McGraw-Hill, 1967.

Chazin, Daniel D. *Hiking Guide to Delaware Water Gap National Recreation Area*. New York: New York–New Jersey Trail Conference, 1994.

Fike, Jean. *Terrestrial & Palustrine Plant Communities of Pennsylvania*. Harrisburg: Pennsylvania Department of Conservation and Natural Resources, 1999.

Freedman, Sally A. *Images of America: Delaware Water Gap the Stroudsburgs and the Poconos*. Dover, NH: Arcadis, 1995.

Gadomski, Michael P. *Reserves of Strength: Pennsylvania's Natural Landscape*. Atglen, PA: Schiffer, 2013.

———. *The Poconos: Pennsylvania's Mountain Treasure*. Atglen, PA: Schiffer, 2015.

Kopczynski, Susan A. *Exploring Delaware Water Gap History: A Field Guide to the Historic Structures and Cultural Landscapes of the Delaware Water Gap National Recreation Area*. Fort Washington, PA: Eastern National, 2000.

Kricher, John C., and Gordon Morrison. *Eastern Forest: Peterson Field Guides*. Boston: Houghton Mifflin, 1988.

Letcher, Gary. *Waterfalls of the Mid-Atlantic States*. Woodstock, VT: Countryman, 2004.

McCabe, Charlotte. *Down the Delaware: A River User's Guide*. Fort Washington, PA: Eastern National, 2003.

McCormick, Jack. *The Life of the Forest*. New York: McGraw-Hill, 1966.

McKnight, Kent H., and Vera B. McKnight. *The Peterson Field Guide Series: A Field Guide to Mushrooms*. Boston: Houghton Mifflin, 1987.

Mitchell, Jeff. *Paddling Pennsylvania: Canoeing and Kayaking the Keystone State's Rivers and Lakes*. Mechanicsburg, PA: Stackpole Books, 2010.

National Geographic Society. *Delaware Water Gap National Recreation Area: Trails Illustrated Topographic Map*. Evergreen, CO: National Geographic Maps, 2013.

New York–New Jersey Trail Conference. Maps 120 to 123. In *Kittatinny Trails: Seventh Edition*. Mahwah, NJ: New York–New Jersey Trail Conference, 2016.

Niering, William A. *The Life of the Marsh: The North American Wetlands*. New York: McGraw-Hill, 1966.

Oplinger, Carl S., and Robert Halma. *The Poconos: An Illustrated Natural History Guide*. New Brunswick, NJ: Rutgers University Press, 1988.

Palmer, Tim. *Twilight of the Hemlocks and Beeches*. University Park, PA: The Pennsylvania State University Press, 2018.

Peterson, Lee. *The Peterson Field Guide Series: A Field Guide to Edible Wild Plants*. Boston: Houghton Mifflin, 1978.

Peterson, Rodger Tory. *Peterson Field Guide to Birds of Eastern and Central North America*. New York: Houghton Mifflin Harcourt, 2010.

Pleasants, Henry. *A Historical Account of the Pocono Region of Pennsylvania*. Philadelphia: John C. Winston, 1913.

Rhoads, Ann Flower, and Timothy A. Block. *Trees of Pennsylvania: A Complete Reference Guide*. Philadelphia: University of Pennsylvania Press, 2005.

Scherer, Glen, and Don Hopey. *Exploring the Appalachian Trail: Hikes in the Mid-Atlantic States*. Mechanicsburg, PA: Stackpole Books, 1998.

Stutz, Bruce. *Natural Lives—Modern Times: People and Places of the Delaware River*. New York: Crown, 1992.

Sutton, George Miksch. *An Introduction to the Birds of Pennsylvania*. Harrisburg, PA: J. Horace McFarland, 1928.

Thieret, John W., and William A. Niering. *The Audubon Society Field Guide to North American Mushrooms*. New York: Alfred A. Knopf, 1981.

Usinger, Robert L. *The Life of Rivers and Streams*. New York: McGraw-Hill, 1967.

Weidensaul, Scott. *Mountains of the Heart: A Natural History of the Appalachians*. Golden, CO: Fulcrum, 2016.

Whiteford, Richard D., and Michael P. Gadomski. *Wild Pennsylvania: A Celebration of Our State's Natural Beauty*. St. Paul, MN: Voyageur, 2006.

WEBSITES

Friends of Marie Zimmerman. "Friends of Marie Zimmermann." Accessed November 26, 2017, www.friendsofmariezimmermann.org.

New Jersey Department of Environmental Protection. "New Jersey Division of Fish & Wildlife." Accessed November 26, 2017, www.nj.gov/dep/fgw/.

Pennsylvania Department of Conservation and Natural Resources. "Trail of Geology Outstanding Geologic Features." Accessed November 26, 2017, http://164.156.186.112/DCNR/topogeo/publications/pgspub/trailgeology/index.htm.

Skylands Visitor. "Guide to Northwest New Jersey." Accessed November 26, 2017, www.njskylands.com.

Sweetman, Jennie. "Thunder Mountain Dude Ranch/Camp to Be Recalled." *New Jersey Herald*, July 9, 2017, www.njherald.com/20170709/thunder-mountain-dude-ranchcamp-to-be-recalled#.

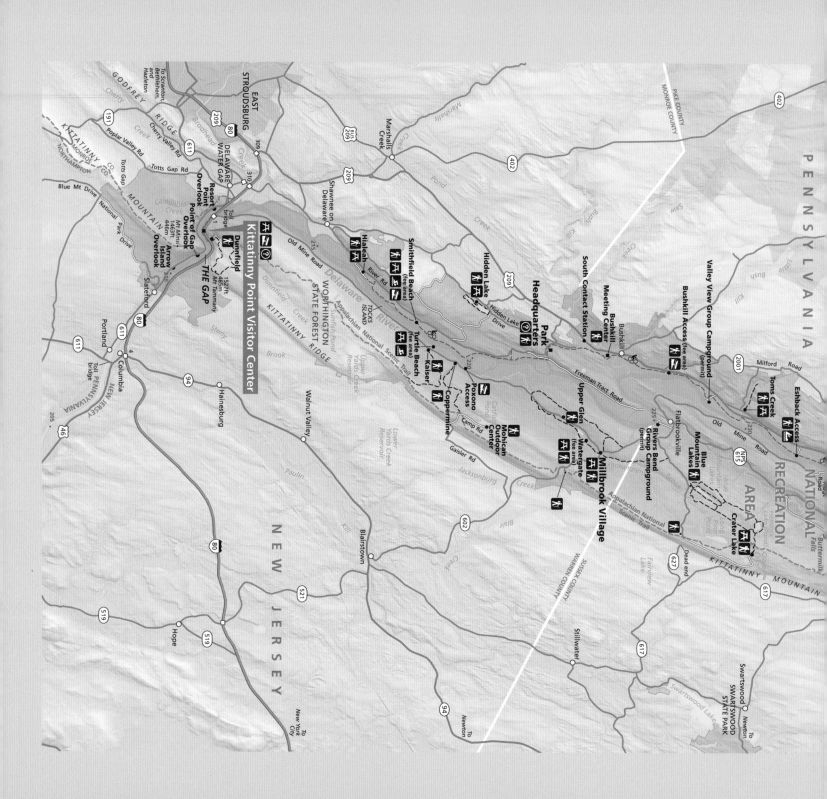